# Travels with Bassem

Cover designed by: Siori Kitajima, SFAppWorks LLC www.sfappworks.com
Formatting by Siori Kitajima and Ovidiu Vlad, SFAppWorks LLC
eBook Formatted by Ovidiu Vlad
Cataloging-in-Publication data for this book is available
from the Library of Congress

ISBN 10: 0991662997
ISBN 13: 978-0-9916629-9-9

Published by The Sager Group LLC
www.TheSagerGroup.Net
info@TheSagerGroup.Net

# Travels with Bassem

## A Palestinian and a Jew Find Friendship in a War-Torn Land

### BY MIKE SAGER

THE SAGER GROUP

Artifex Te Adiuva

# Editor's note

*Some of the names in this story
have been changed.*

*This book was made possible
by grants from Vicki Vance
and The Sager Group LLC
as a memorial to Bassem Hallak,
whose love, friendship, and
devotion to his native Palestine
will always be cherished.*

# Introduction

Bassem Salim Hallak was the son of Salim Hallak, a barber and shop owner in the Old City of Jerusalem. Like his father, he was born in Jerusalem. According to family records, the Hallak family goes back more than 10 generations in Jerusalem.

Bassem's mother, Feryall, was born in Lebanon. According to family lore, Salim Hallak frequently went to Lebanon on business. One day, he spotted Feryall going into school. He tracked down her family and proposed marriage. She was only 14 when they were married. Salim was about 28.

Bassem was the third of 10 children - all born in Jerusalem. He attended schools all over Jerusalem and Ramallah—and was kicked out of nearly every one, much to the dismay of his father. While Bassem was not a champion student, after his father's death, he did his best to make sure that the rest of his siblings continued their higher education (and they all did). Until the end he was devoted to his mother.

Around age 14, Bassem, like many Palestinian boys of that era, became involved in the struggle, the Palestinian Intifada. During this time he was a golden gloves boxer, in the lightweight category. Also during this time he was first arrested and served time in jail. Bassem liked to joke that Jewish boys were Bar Mitzvah and Palestinian boys were thrown in jail – both events signified manhood in their respective cultures, he said.

Bassem was always frank about his involvement as an organizer of the first Intifada. He was known by some as the "flag of Palestine" during these years because of his unwavering conviction and seeming fearlessness in the face of arrest. He spent many years in and out of prison for political activity and fighting with soldiers.

During the first Intifada, Bassem helped coordinate classes for students when the schools were closed, and food deliveries to homes when the shops were on strike. He also helped organize many marches and demonstrations, including the early children's marches, and worked as a translator and press aide to reporters covering the clashes. Because of a warrant issued for his arrest after the first Intifada collapsed, he spent a few years in Europe – primarily in Germany, but also Italy and Switzerland. He soon became homesick. As soon as the opportunity arose, he headed home. He believed it was his right and duty to live in the land of his birth.

Upon his return to Jerusalem, Bassem opened his own shop on the Villa Dolarosa specializing in Palestinian antiquities and jewelry. Before him, his paternal grandmother had done a thriving business renting diamonds and other antique jewelry for weddings and other important occasions. It was through her that Bassem learned the beginnings of what he knew about antiques, jewelry and Palestinian cultural heritage. Her guidance and example sparked a love of his trade that never waned.

Around 2000, Bassem went to work for a German NGO that sent teams of doctors into war torn countries to provide health care services. Bassem was instrumental in establishing a Jerusalem office which spearheaded the set-up of the first mobile clinic to deliver health care services throughout the West Bank and Gaza. Bassem connected hospitals with volunteer teams of physicians, surgeons, and nurses. As a result, urgent care and needed surgeries were delivered to thousands of Palestinian children. When critical cases required treatment in Germany, Bassem secured funding and accommodations for their trips, and also helped secure travel and return visas for the children and their parents.

During his entire life, Bassem remained steadfastly dedicated to the establishment of a Palestinian state with full rights for all of its inhabitants. He was often referred to as the unofficial "mayor" of Jerusalem. He cared for and helped raise many for the young men of the old city, reminding them of their history and the responsibilities they bore facing an uncertain future. On any given day you could find city residents coming and going from Bassem's shop in the old city. Often sought after for his wisdom—and sometimes despised for his honestly and love of the truth—Bassem was called upon to settle disputes between shop keepers, youngsters in the neighborhood, and neighborhood friends. Every Ramadan, in the tradition of sharing, he and a few other men hosted a special dinner for the neighborhood.

A few weeks before his death Bassem physically put himself between a young boy and a group of settlers who were allegedly intent on kidnapping the boy. The confrontation caused soldiers and others to come running from all quarters of the city. Eventually a commander, who knew Bassem from the days of the first intifada, arrived on the scene and diffused tensions.

Bassem died at age 54 in his family's home on the Mount of Olives while awaiting an ambulance. Over the next three days, more than 1500 people arrived to pay their respects. If the borders between the West Bank and Gaza had been open there would have been at least double the number.

# Travels with Bassem

BASSEM IS CALLING, collect from Jerusalem. He's been missing for two weeks. I've been worried.

The line hiccups and clicks, spits static. Then I hear his voice.

"They arrested me," he says, the accent thick, a tone of outrage. "Right after you left, they take me from my house. They put me in jail. The whole time I just sit there like an animal. They didn't even ask me one single question. Then they let me go. Just like that. They are really after something, Mike. I don't know what it is."

The words skip across the ocean like hard, flat stones. I was afraid something like this would happen. Bassem and I went through a lot. I keep his picture on my desk, a five by seven glossy in a simple Lucite frame. I look at it while he speaks.

He is sitting, right knee crossed over left, on a pile of Bedouin rugs beside a tray of trinket earrings, in his family's shop in the Old City. He's wearing designer jeans, a silk shirt, a gold chain, white socks, tan loafers. Though he is looking straight at the camera, his eyes, one of which is set deeper than the other, seem to be saying two different things. The right one is focused and wary; it is in his world right now, a place where anything can happen at any moment. The left one appears unfocused and wistful, dreamy and far away. It seems to be in another place, a place that may never be.

In these weeks since my return from Israel, I have looked often at Bassem's picture, for there is much to remember, even more to try and comprehend. Bassem showed me Israel, his Israel, a place he calls Palestine. He translated Arabic and Hebrew into English for me, got me a discount on a rental car, invited me home, fed me his mother's stuffed grape leaves, guided me to illegal places, floated with me at midnight in the Dead Sea, beneath a million ancient stars. We drove all over the country; he took me to meet his friends. There was Ziad, the Bedouin accountant. His family's lone remaining camel was tied to a stake in the middle of their compound—under Israeli law, the Bedouins were no longer allowed to roam the desert. Naser was a civil engineer. He made water pipes out of irrigation tubing stolen from Israeli settlements. Mohammed was a graduate of the Bethlehem University School of Hotel Management. Poona lived in Dahisha, the oldest of the refugee camps. Her neighbors called her Mother of the Camp; she served us endless rounds of orange soda, mint tea, Turkish coffee. Samir, in Gaza, had a seventeen-year-old Peugeot with a trunk full of cruddy tires. He'd stop here and there and chat a while, leave a tire behind. Later, the tire would be burned, a crude roadblock, a feeble but symbolic attempt to keep out Israeli soldiers. Taher rented a room in the Jerusalem that was seven hundred years old. Every morning before work, he rode his Exercycle, listened to reggae music on his headphones.

Bassem did a lot of things to help me; he saved my ass and I saved his. And though I paid him a good wage to be my translator, he wasn't in my service. (From time to time, in fact, I had the distinct impression that I was in his.) From that day in the West Bank, when the soldier cocked his M-16 and commanded us to come or die, Bassem and I were friends. "This is the life," Bassem would say, when we were stopped at a checkpoint, when we visited wounded boys in the hospital, when the soldiers threatened to beat us, when the refugees ran us out of the camp, when the Israeli waiter pretended we didn't exist, when we had to stay inside for days at a time because a town was under curfew. Bassem shared the life with me. He let me in.

Now he is on the phone, collect from Jerusalem. He's in trouble. There is nothing I can do.

"Mike," he says, "you can't even believe this. Ziad is arrested. And Samir, he is arrested too. Mohammed is in the hospital. He is unconscious. The doctors cut off his right arm.

"I think they were following us, Mike. In Gaza. In Hebron. In Akko. In Bethlehem. But it is not only this.

Even in the American Colony Hotel. Remember the pho-
tographer? The men in the garden? I have to go see my
lawyer. I have to talk to some people. They are really up
to something. I have to find out what it is."

\* \* \*

The plane rolled to a stop in the middle of the runway at
Ben Gurion Airport, far from any buildings, and everyone
clapped and chanted prayers. Late June 1988. A flight to
Tel Aviv, full of Jews. Blonde Jews and bearded Jews, Jews
with videocams, Jews in fur-covered hats, Jews speaking
Spanish, English, French, Russian—all of them making
*aliya,* the blessed return to the Promised land, a right and
a privilege bestowed by both the Torah and the State of
Israel.

Myself, I was a Jew making *aliya* on assignment. It
was my first trip to Israel. I'd been warned. Be careful of
danger, they said. Be careful what you write: There are
larger considerations at stake. I gathered my knapsack
and my trepidations and walked up the aisle, stepped
through the hatch. The sun was already strong. The wind
blew grit. I put on my sunglasses, waited my turn behind
grandmothers and kids.

Down the gangway, two steps on tarmac.

A beefy guy started hollering. He pointed at me, came
running in my direction. Four others followed.

I was surrounded: Three men, two women, all of
them wearing identical sport shirts and chinos. The first
guy jabbered at me in Arabic. Another reached slowly for

the bulge beneath his shirt. There was panic in his mirrored sunglasses, my reflection...

Things were not well in Israel. For the past seven months, the *Intifada*, the Struggle, had been raging in the territories seized during the Six-Day War of 1967. Beginning in December of 1987, the two million Arabs indigenous to the territories, the Palestinians, had erupted spontaneously in mass protest. Local committees were formed. Children and mothers were demonstrating. An ordered, primitive, effective, grassroots uprising was taking place on the front pages of major newspapers around the world. The Palestinians protested and struck and built roadblocks, threw stones at the formidable Israeli troops. The soldiers, great-grandchildren of the Holocaust, countered with tear gas and automatic weapons, the bullets sometimes rubber, sometimes real.

Since the Intifada began, two hundred Palestinians had died, two Israelis had died. Thousands of Palestinians, the majority of them teenagers, had been shot or beaten. More than fifteen thousand Palestinians had been arrested; at least fifteen hundred were being held without charge on "administrative detention" by edict of military commanders. More than thirty Palestinian houses had been destroyed. Long the victims, the Jews were beginning to look like the oppressors. The Palestinian terrorist on the six o'clock news was beginning to look a lot younger. And he was beginning to look like the good guy.

Clearly, Israel was troubled. Born in 1948 into a state of war, faced always with the possibility of extinction, the Jewish homeland had grown, but she had not matured. The institutions set up forty years earlier in a state of military alert were still in place, but they no longer accommodated the needs of the burgeoning, modern nation that Israel had become. Over the years, ad hoc had become status quo. The Israelis hadn't even gotten around yet to writing a constitution.

In the coming six weeks, while I was in-country, Israeli doctors would call a full-fledged strike and all ambulance service would be suspended. The nation's district court judges would threaten to resign "en bloc" in a dispute over a Knesset plan to reorganize the court system. Jewish factory workers would storm the Ministry of Finance, wielding clubs in protest of government plans to lay off almost three hundred. The Education Minister would warn the cabinet that because of budget cuts, "the Israelis are gradually becoming a nation of mediocrities." The Central Bureau of Statistics would report a $1.3 billion decline in share value on the Tel Aviv stock exchange for the first six months of 1988.

The country, its systems, its institutions, even the buildings in its hastily assembled model city, Tel Aviv, were crumbling around the edges from neglect. A raucous national election was in progress. The nation was traumatized and split by the dirty war of attrition in the territories. Neighboring Arab countries were announcing arms deals with China and France. The war between Iran and Iraq was heading toward a truce; the lull in headlines was sure to focus even more attention on the plight of the Palestinians. King Hussein of Jordan was about to absolve himself of responsibility for the Palestinians in the occupied territories, leaving the United States and Israel faced with the almost certain possibility that the Palestine Liberation Organization would have to be recognized if negotiations were ever to convene. The world—even the U.S., even some American Jews—was beginning to lose patience with the stark, ugly news footage of soldiers shooting at children. "Our relations with many countries have been reduced to the level of constant justification," a Foreign Ministry official would be quoted as saying.

And so it was that my plane landed at Ben Gurion and I was surrounded by plainclothes government agents, one reaching for his gun. Everything on the airfield had screeched to a halt and everyone was staring—the passengers on the gangway, the stewardesses, the baggage handlers, the engineers, old and young, Spanish and French and American and Israeli—all of them Jews, all of them scared to death, sure that their worst fears were coming true and that any moment I was going to run amok or take hostages or commence firing or blowing something up.

I removed my shades, raised my hands in surrender. I'm short, dark and bearded, wear an earring in my left ear. Like many Jewish men, I am half-bald on the top. Unlike many, I complete nature's work with a razor. At home, my friends often joke that I look like a terrorist.

At the moment, it didn't seem so funny anymore.

"It's okay, I'm Jewish!" I said, forcing a smile. "No problem! I'm Jewish!"

Two other agents went for their guns.

\* \* \*

Bassem is calling, collect from Jerusalem.

"Mike, everything is shit," he says.

"The other day I was threatened by the Israelian security. They saw me in Salahadin Street. They say, 'You're out of prison, but don't think you are as free as you really think. We know what you are doing. We're just waiting for the right time and the right charge. This is your end, that's it.'

"I cannot stay here. I need to go someplace for a few months so my name will be forgotten here, or not even to be forgotten, but for things to start quieting down. They are putting this chain around my neck. They are making it tighter. I don't know what to do."

\* \* \*

At sundown on Sabbath the Old City glowed; the muezzin at the mosque sang a strange nasal sura. Three boys in shorts and kneesocks and long black coats hurried through the Arab Quarter, arm in arm in arm, sidecurls flying beneath wide-brimmed hats. Leaves of cardamom and pieces of trash skittered across the narrow cobbled streets, which echoed the ancient, solitary clip-clop of a donkey. Soldiers clustered in archways on folding chairs, guns in laps. On the Via Dolorosa, where Christ carried his cross, a man in a long, dress-like *jalabia* carried a refrigerator on his back.

The Jews call this city *Yerushalayim*, the City of Peace. The Arabs call it *al-Quds*, the Holy. Set along a ridge of strong stone hills the color of sand, Old Jerusalem is a fortress behind a thick, saw-toothed wall. To the east is the desert, the land of milk. To the west is the fertile plain, the land of honey. For four thousand years, men have fought over the ownership of Jerusalem. It is the city where David ruled, where Christ died, where Mohammed ascended. The streets here are mentioned in the Bible; you can stand in places where miracles occurred. Jerusalem stands as a monument to the religious beliefs of half the people on Earth. Since its beginnings as a Canaanite city-state in the Bronze Age, Jerusalem has been ruled, alternately, by Jews, Macedonians, Egyptians, Seleucids, Greeks, Jewish Hasmoneans, Romans, Byzantines, Persians, Umayyads, Abbasids, Fatimids, Ayyubids, Crusaders, Mameluks, Ottoman Turks, British, Jordanians, and now again the Jews.

I was headed out of the Old City, through the Arab Quarter, toward the Damascus Gate. I'd been to the Wailing Wall for the Friday evening service.

I'd climbed up high near a barbed wire fence to watch. At the Wall, black hats and yarmulkes bobbed in prayer. Behind them, tourists circled guides. The name of God was spoken in many languages. Young soldiers cruised the massive courtyard, scanning for trouble, scoping the foreign girls. The Wall itself is one hundred feet high. It is made of great blocks of Herodian stone. Actually, it's a retaining wall: it holds back the western face of Mount Moria, the Temple Mount. Over a period of one thousand years, in a repeating pattern of defeat, exile, and return, the Jews laid claim to this hallowed plateau, a reign by the God of Israel that ended in 70 AD, when the Roman emperor Titus destroyed the Second Temple and slaughtered and enslaved the Jews.

High above the soldiers, worshippers, and tourists, above the Wall itself, on that very same hallowed plateau, the gold Dome of the Rock hunkers beneath an Arab crescent. The Al Aqsa mosque was built in 691 AD. It is the third most sacred site in all of Islam. One of the duties of a good Muslim is to make three pilgrimages in his lifetime—to Mecca and Medina in Saudi Arabia, and to Jerusalem, to this mosque. At the heart of the complex is a huge, tan-colored rock formation, the exact place where Mohammed mounted his winged steed and flew to heaven to meet Allah. To this day, in bas relief in the rock, you can see Mohammed's footprint. Hanging above it is a glass canister. Inside are three hairs from the prophet's beard.

I'd just arrived in Jerusalem from Tel Aviv. I'd been in Israel four days. Being here, among my people, was not like being in other foreign countries. Everything was so familiar. I didn't know the language, but I was fluent in the customs. Everything about the place was Jewish. The restaurants had all the stuff we used to eat only on holidays. The faces of the Jewish people reminded me of every Jewish face I'd ever known. The words in people's sentences were the same words I used in the prayers I'd said as a kid, only they were using them to talk about the weather. I had this strange feeling, like someone had taken all my furniture and arranged it exactly the same way in a different room.

But it was more than that. The way the lady in the hotel bookstore admonished the eleven-year-old who was paging through a *Hustler* magazine: "What do you know from such trash?" she said, shooing him with both hands out the door. The way the older man in the sundries shop, after I told him I didn't need a bag for my postcards, urged, "Take it, it's better in a bag." The way the hotel operator had admonished: "There's nothing wrong with the phone. It must be you."

In Fodor's guide to Israel, the 1988 edition, it is explained that Jews are "generally warm, friendly, generous people. They can also be prying, rude and exasperating." I guess I would have to agree. It's how the world thinks of us; it's how I think of us too. My best friends from college were Jews from Long Island. It could be said, with apologies to them, that they were prime examples of the archetypal ugly American Jew: gold chains, loud mouths, a certain air of entitlement. Becoming close friends with these guys helped me learn a very important lesson: Someone can act like a jerk but still be a great guy. It's an extension, I suppose, of something my parents taught: you can love someone even if you don't like what they do.

You need to know these things in Israel, if only to acclimate yourself to the attitude. It is part of the heritage, the upbringing—the way Jewish kids are taught that they are loved, that they are special. Jews like themselves. They have great amounts of self-esteem. They believe they can accomplish things. It has something to do with the religion, I believe. Jews aren't born encumbered with an original sin; we don't start life with a theological strike against us. We do, however, start life with a cultural strike against us.

My parents always had a keen sense of their Jewishness, and I suppose I have it too. Both grew up in small towns in Virginia. Things were not easy. Some of their neighbors actually believed they had horns.

"It was mostly verbal stuff," my dad has said. "Damn Jew, damn kike. Something that would come up. But it was more than that. It was the idea that was hard. They never forgot you were a Jew, and they never let you forget either. You couldn't be a Jew and be part of the rest of the world too. That's how they made me feel."

After they were married, when I was young, my parents moved to Baltimore, to Pikesville, a neighborhood the Jews themselves called a "golden ghetto." There were six temples along a two-mile stretch of Park Heights Avenue; growing up, no one ever made me feel like there was something inherently wrong with my existence on the planet. But no matter where you grow up Jewish, you're made to remember—from the slaves in Egypt to the death camps in Nazi Germany—how it has always been for your people, what it means to be Jewish.

Now I was in the Jewish homeland, a member of the majority. Walking back to my hotel from Sabbath services at the holiest of Jewish places, the Wailing Wall, I headed along a narrow street in the Arab Quarter of the Old City of Jerusalem, filled with the odd sensation that, for once in my life, I was in a place where being Jewish was actually an advantage.

Up ahead, however, there were nothing but Arabs. The street was dark, close, menacing. Men smoked and played cards. Little boys played soccer and rode bikes. My leather sandals, bought that day in the market, clicked too loudly on the cobbles. As I came closer, everything stopped.

Then someone yelled at me: "Hey Kojak!"

A chorus erupted: "Kojak! Kojak! Kojak!"

In those days before Michael Jordan, a shaved head was something you didn't see every day. The little ones surrounded me, and they laughed and pointed, and then one of them got the courage to touch my head with his fingertips, and then all of them, maybe twenty young boys in all, began to reach and touch and laugh, squealing "Kojak! Kojak! Kojak!" referring, of course, to the popular TV detective with the shaved head, available in Israel in reruns. A boy named Nasser spoke a little English. He asked me to give him five, and I did, slapping his palm at waist level. Then I taught him a new way, and everyone took turns slapping palms high in the air.

Nasser locked his fingers in mine, walked me over to some older guys who were sitting around drinking tea outside a store called Holy City Souvenirs. He introduced me to everyone, and most rose in turn to shake my hand. One, however, refused to rise. Like the rest, he was wearing designer jeans and an expensive-looking tapered dress shirt, open almost to his navel. He nodded in my direction, barely cordial.

I took a seat with the men and little Nasser brought me sweet mint tea. The boys gathered around. We drank and smoked cigarettes, talked of this and that in broken English. Then Nasser made his close.

"You want to buy something in shop?"

"I am not here to buy," I explained politely. "I'm a journalist. You understand journalist?"

They understood. There was much to tell.

One boy spoke about his two brothers in prison. Another showed me his broken arm, made chop-chop motions like a billy club—the other tool of the soldiers— across the plaster cast with his good hand. A third pulled a picture from his wallet, his dead cousin. A fourth pulled a picture from his pocket, his dead brother.

Their litany was long and horrifying, even in broken English. Houses demolished, land stolen, children shot, babies dead from tear gas. "The Jewish do this," each repeated in turn. "The Jewish."

I was gut-shot. I had no idea. This was 1988, seven months into the Intifada. No one had any idea, not really. No one outside of Palestine, anyway.

The stories continued until well after dark. I didn't have my tape recorder with me. "Maybe I should come back tomorrow," I said. "Maybe we can talk some more?"

Everyone looked to the skeptical guy. He was in his late twenties, roughly the same age as me. He was sitting on a pile of Bedouin rugs. He hadn't said a word all evening. He stroked his moustache, looked me up and down. Finally, he spoke:

"Mr. Mike," he said, with much formality. "Are you, by chance, a Jewish?"

\* \* \*

Palestinians have this way of making you wait. They say they'll call on Saturday afternoon, so you wait in your room until Saturday night. On Sunday, you wait in the garden courtyard of the hotel, running back and forth to the front desk to remind them to transfer the call. You wait three hours and drink six cups of thick Turkish coffee, and then you go the bathroom.

That's when they call.

And they leave an admonishing message.

So it was on my third day in Jerusalem. I was waiting for a call back from a Palestinian urologist.

An organization in Washington, DC, the American Arab Anti-Discrimination Committee, had set me up with the doctor. The idea was that I—the son of a Jewish gynecologist—would live with him and his family for a week or two, experience upper-middle-class life in the occupied territories. I'd had this notion that the world didn't really see Palestinians as people. They were an issue. They were politics. They were numbers, quotes and footage. But there was never any sense of them as human beings.

I'd met some Palestinians in Washington before I left. When I thought about it, they seemed a lot like Jews. They valued family and education. Many were well off. People hated them. They had their own Diaspora—college-educated Palestinians were settled all over the Arab world; they held the kind of important, background positions that Jews have always held. Palestinian kids are taught that they are loved, that they are special. Palestinians like themselves. They have lots of self-esteem. They believe they can accomplish things. I wondered if maybe this was a clue to what was happening in Israel. As time went on, I would form this picture in my mind: someone boxing his own mirror image.

And so it was that I, the son of a Jewish gynecologist, had arranged to stay with a Palestinian urologist and his family in the West Bank. Now, if I only could divine at what hour on which day he would choose to return my call, I could begin my research in earnest.

I was staying in Arab East Jerusalem, in the stately oasis of neutrality called the American Colony Hotel. Built in 1840 for a Turkish pasha and his four wives, it was a ten-minute walk from the Damascus Gate. In 1917, the Arab mayor of Jerusalem used one of the American Colony's white sheets to surrender to the British army. In 1948, during the war for Israeli independence, the owner of the hotel turned the lobby into a hospital. In 1967, the hotel was caught in the crossfire of the Six-Day War, taking more than twenty direct hits during the battle for East Jerusalem. More recently, U.S. Secretary of State George Shultz had scheduled a meeting here with Palestinian leaders, a first tiny step toward recognition of the "outlaw" regime as a legitimate voice of the people.

Those Palestinians kept him waiting too. Indefinitely.

Now, sitting in the garden courtyard of the American Colony Hotel, I was drinking another coffee, reading the introduction to a book called *Arab and Jew*, written by Pulitzer Prize winner David K. Shipler in 1986.

"This is the land most burdened and enriched by history, most scarred and coveted by the Jews and Arabs who now face each other in combat, in distaste, in regard, in accommodation, in strange affinity," it said. "Both peoples are victims. Each has suffered at the hands of the outsiders, and each has been wounded by the other."

The Jews, he said, "have been subordinated, despised, vilified, imprisoned and slaughtered. Throughout their history, they have been haunted by a corrosive sense of illegitimacy... And they have stood and fallen alone. Nobody has rescued them except incidentally, as the Allies liberated many from the concentration camps after defeating Hitler's Germany."

The Palestinians, he continued—in a passage written some two years before the Intifada began—have "suffered powerlessness and deprivation of liberty but never genocide. Their sense of distinctiveness as a Palestinian people has come not from an ancient source but largely in reaction to the creation and growth of Israel on part of the land where they lived. In contemporary, personal terms, then, many Palestinian Arabs have been the victims of expulsion, displacement and war. They have found themselves scattered and rejected in the Arab world at large."

"Is this how you report your story, Mr. Mike? You sit in the garden of the hotel and read a book?"

I twisted around. It was the skeptical guy from the Arab Quarter.

Over the last few days, in between bouts of waiting for Dr. Jibril to call, I'd gone back to Holy City Souvenirs. I can't say I was welcomed, exactly. The older guys I'd first met didn't want to talk anymore. The skeptical guy made a point of not even noticing me. I don't think he'd believed me when I told him I was Greek—just like Kojak. Mostly, I'd spent my time with little Nasser. He took me around the old city, showing me the sights, stopping here and there for a high-five. I certainly hadn't told anyone where I was staying.

"Well, see," I stuttered, trying to explain, "there's this Palestinian doctor—"

"Let me tell you something Mr. Mike—" he motioned to the chair, raised his eyebrows. "May I sit down?"

He said his name was Bassem. I reached over and shook his hand. He crossed his legs, looked around the garden restaurant. It was nearly empty. "A few months ago," he said, "if you came to this hotel, hundreds of journalists were here. Upstairs, downstairs, in the garden, in the restaurant. They were all of them from press. They thought the Intifada was going to last for three months, or even two, or even four months. And then, after four months, they start asking, 'What are we doing here?' They are fed up with it.

"To them, it was only a matter of very important news. They want to be famous. They want to show their people back in their country, 'Look, I got this story. I'm a good reporter or even I can be a famous reporter.' For them, it's a chance to get a big story, to get lots of attention for himself, especially if he is a young reporter, like you."

I raised my hand in protest, but he continued. "Mr. Mike, I have been watching you. I have seen you in the Old City. I have seen you here and there. But I have never once seen you with a camera. I have never once seen you writing things down. I have never once heard you ask any questions."

Bassem looked at me for a long moment. He shook his head slowly. *Tisk, tisk.* I didn't know what to say.

"I have decided," he said at last, flourishing his hand in the air like a sheik ordering the dancing girls. "I will get you your story, Mike. I will get you a *very* good story. You can count on me."

\* \* \*

Bassem is calling, collect from Zurich.

"How did you get out?" I ask.

"I used a travel document."

"They gave you a travel document?"

"I pay money to get it. There is an Arab man who work for security. I go through him. Then, when I went to the airport, they stopped me. They say I can't leave the country. They say I have to bring this paper from the court.

"I need this file from 1982, so the next morning, I go to the court. I go from office to office, from place to place. Nobody's willing to help, nobody's willing to listen. Everybody was using his phone, everybody was having a meeting, no one would say anythings to me. It took me three fucking days to get the paper.

"And you know, the second time I come to the airport, they never even mention this paper! But they did search me. Ten times they search me. Three times they make me take off my clothes. I told them listen, I'm very offended to this."

"What are you going to do now?"

"I have no plan yet," he says. "I need to go to Germany, and then I will have a plan. I need to see the country. I don't think I can live in such places like this. It is something to do with the view you see around here, the kind of country it is. Everything not right here. This is not what I am used to. It is imitation to me. It is not like Jerusalem. Nothing's real."

\* \* \*

At three in the afternoon on a stifling day in early July, three months earlier, Bassem and I were speeding down the highway, through Ramallah in the West Bank, driving back to Jerusalem. Dry, dusty wind whistled though the windows of my rented Renault. Scenery eddied over the asphalt; silence baked between us. Past watermelon stands, donkey carts. Everywhere seemed deserted.

"Look at this!" Bassem exclaimed. "Park over there."

The sun bleached the hills, scorched the backs of our necks. We scrambled down a rocky embankment, stood behind a waist-high wall. Five hundred yards away, down in the valley, a rock-strewn road through a little village, a truck full of Israeli soldiers.

Three of the soldiers had set a perimeter—points north, east, and west from the truck. A fourth directed a work party of civilians. A young boy and a woman wearing a veil worked together to roll a medium-sized boulder to the side of the road. Six teenagers attempted to pull a burned-out car from a gully. Others swept and picked up stones.

"This is how they clean the streets," Bassem whispered. "They go to the houses and take the people out. They make them take down the rocks and the barricades. When the soldiers leave, the people put them back up."

"What's the point?"

"This is what means *occupation*. The soldiers have to drive through the village one time or maybe two times every day. Then they can say they are occupying, or even that they are in control. When the soldiers come, the demonstration comes."

"So if the soldiers didn't come in, the people wouldn't riot?"

"Yesssss, Miiiike." It was tone I had come to know well, reserved for such occasions as this, dripping irony, a song of the obvious.

"Let's get closer," I said. I swung a leg over the wall.

"TAL!" shouted a soldier, the one on the northern perimeter. We'd been spotted.

"What is he saying?" I asked

"He says to come."

"Do you think we should?"

"If this is what you like to do, Mike."

"TAL!" the soldier repeated. Then he cocked his rifle. You could hear it five hundred yards away, the familiar metallic *click-shick* of lock and load. He raised the weapon, fit it to his shoulder. It was American-made, an M-16. He laid his cheek to the stock and aimed…

I approached holding my press cards high overhead, dancing them on the chain. The soldier kept his rifle shouldered. He yelled something in Arabic.

"I speak English," I said indignantly to the barrel of his loaded weapon. "If you want to speak to me, speak in English! I'm American!"

We'd spent the morning visiting the wounded of the Intifada, a hospital in the old Arab city of Nablus. I met a fourteen-year-old with a bullet hole in his back, a seven-year-old with a cluster of three bullet wounds in his calf—Olympic-caliber marksmanship. I met kids with broken arms and legs and missing eyes. I learned that a so-called "rubber bullet" was really a solid cylinder of lead with a rubber coating around it. A twelveyear-old had taken two rubber bullets to the face at close range. The damage was indescribable.

One ten-year-old had taken a bullet in the thigh. The artery had been shredded; the leg was gangrenous. I stood at the end of the bed with my tape recorder. "Are you scared?"

The boy's lip quivered. "No," he squeaked.

I had to leave the room.

The hospital, called Al Itihad, was run by the Arab Women's Union. It was a charity hospital, one of the few in the territories that was operated, staffed, and funded totally by Palestinians. It had space for sixty beds. Already, they'd squeezed in ninety-two.

That very morning the Israeli government had announced new rules for medical care for Palestinians. Starting today, any Palestinian who went to the Israelis for treatment would have to pay in advance for three days' care. If you participated in a demonstration, for instance, and were shot by a soldier, it would cost you about a thousand dollars—up front—to receive emergency treatment.

The new medical rules were part of larger plan. Besides the obvious measures invoked under the Israelis' new "iron fist" policies—the midnight searches of houses, the billy clubs and rubber bullets, the internal espionage, the administrative detentions, the torture, the deportations—the Israelis were laying siege to the Palestinian economy. Subtly, surgically, they were cutting the flow of resources to the territories.

Sometimes the government would turn off the telephones. Sometimes they'd cut the water or the electricity, or stop the shipments of fuel. Already they'd shut down several Palestinian produce markets, cut international communications, and imposed restrictions on travel, on building houses, and on the amount of foreign currency an Arab could bring into the territories. Hundreds of thousands of Jordanian dinars and American dollars had been seized at Ben Gurion Airport and at the Allenby Bridge, the crossing from Amman.

Towns, villages, cities and refugee camps were intermittently put under curfew. When I was there, Jalazun, a refugee camp, had been under curfew for more than a month. On any given day in June or July, eight or ten or fourteen different locations were under military siege, declared "Closed Military Areas" by the regional command. Journalists were turned away at checkpoints many kilometers down the road; sitting in the garden at the American Colony, reporters joked about playing a game called "Hunting the Intifada." You drove around, played hide-and-seek with the soldiers, trying to see for yourself what was going on.

Under curfew, all entrances to Palestinian towns or refugee camps were sealed. Nothing was allowed in, including food, and no one inside moved. People shuttered the windows and sat still, stayed in one room. Men and women relieved themselves in jars and pots, afraid even to cross the open courtyards of their houses for fear of Israeli sentries posted on the roofs nearby.

The government was also cracking down on tax scofflaws. The Palestinians were withholding tax payments on the basis that their money was being used to finance the war against them. But the Israelis controlled the roads; all drivers in the occupied territories had to pass through military checkpoints. Soldiers were checking tax rolls. Cars were being seized on the spot as payment. In some areas, like Gaza, there were hardly any autos left on the road.

Perhaps the most powerful weapon yielded by the Israelis was the "Identicard." By law, every Palestinian had to be registered. The cards—made of paper and holstered in a shirt-pocket-sized plastic sleeve—contained a picture, a name, an address, and a registration number, which corresponded to a central file in Tel Aviv. Failure to have an Identicard in possession could mean immediate arrest. Often, soldiers would drive through a village, round up a work party, confiscate Identicards, leave for an hour or so. The soldiers knew that the Palestinians, Intifada notwithstanding, wouldn't move an inch without their Identicards. It was another little tweak, another indignity, the same same as pissing off the roof in plain sight of a Muslim woman, or throwing rocks at kids from the machine gun nest. In July, one youth in the West Bank would die when a large rock fell off a roof where a soldier was sitting. The death was ruled accidental. It was that kind of confrontation—deep and mean.

All of which, I suppose, had made me angry and ashamed. All of which made me speak to the Jewish soldier the way I did, despite the fact that he was holding a weapon.

I wanted to make something perfectly clear to him. I wanted him to know that I am American, that he couldn't fuck with me because I have a country to protect me.

One of the jobs of a country, if you believe in Rousseau's social contract, is to stand up and claim each citizen as her own. He is mine, the country says to all the other countries in the world. If you have a problem with him, you have to deal with me.

The Palestinians have no country. They have no stamps, no currency, no law, no police, no passport, no Olympic team. They have a flag, but it is outlawed. They have a government, but it is in exile. They have leaders of the Intifada, but they are hiding. There is nothing Palestinian, except people. There is no country to bestow and defend their rights. In the grand historical game of musical chairs, the band has stopped, and there is a nation of people who can't sit down.

And so it was that the soldier jacked us up, and I stood on my American rights, and the guy took the gun out of my face. The lieutenant called us over to the truck. The soldier walked behind.

Upon closer inspection, the truck was actually some kind of lightly armored personnel carrier, It had huge, tractor-like wheels and an open cab, behind which was a flatbed holding two long benches of soldiers, all of them slouched in the shade of an olive drab canvas awning. The lieutenant was up front, in the passenger seat, high off the ground. He dangled a black boot over the side.

I told him I was a journalist, and that Bassem was my translator. I told him we were just touring the area.

The lieutenant said we had to leave. "You will make a riot. It is because of press that the Arabs riot."

I had no camera, no shoulder bag. My tape recorder was in my pocket, and it was running, but no one could see. I did not look like a journalist. "Why would people riot?" I asked.

"You will make a riot. You have to leave," he shot back. Then he snapped his fingers at Bassem, turned his palm up. Bassem handed up his Identicard.

The lieutenant studied it a moment. "You live in Jerusalem?" he asked. "What are you doing here?"

Bassem smiled, a shit-eating grin. "Ramallah is a beautiful town. There is nice breeze here, lieutenant."

"Tell this story to your grandmother," the lieutenant said disdainfully.

"This is the story I have," Bassem shrugged.

The lieutenant spit. "This is a Closed Military Area," he declared.

"No it's not," piped a soldier from the back of the truck.

The lieutenant twisted around on his high seat and muttered something. Then he turned back to us. He pitched Bassem's Identicard into the desert. It flew like a Frisbee.

He leveled us with a menacing stare. "The other day," he growled, "we beat up three journalists, and we beat up two translators. We put them in the hospital. If I see you here again, you two will not be so lucky. You will not make it to the hospital alive."

* * *

"Why should I clean up the streets?" Bassem was saying. "I don't even clean up my own room."

We were on the porch of his family's concrete house in the Mount of Olives, sitting in metal chairs beneath an arbor of green grapes, talking with Bassem's little brother Omar. Omar was 16, the baby. His mother wanted him to be a doctor. He and Bassem shared a room. They were very close.

Thirty years old, Bassem still lived at home, as do most unmarried Palestinian men. Though he sometimes rankled at the arrangement, considering himself a modern sort who would someday occupy his own bachelor pad, he had put his own plans on hold for the time being, in favor of keeping an eye on his little brother. Omar went to private school, was fluent in French and English, liked Hemingway, Camus, Madonna, and George Michael. He wore Pub aftershave, though didn't yet shave, and used Brylcreem in his auburn hair, which he combed in a rakish dip over this right eyebrow. Omar dressed like a kid from the American suburbs: Lee brand stonewashed denims, unlaced Aviva high-tops, oversize T-shirts with the sleeves rolled up over his biceps. A year or so ago, Bassem came home to find Omar had decorating their room with posters of Rambo, Ralph Maccio, Knight Rider, Samantha Fox. He'd scribbled graffiti on the walls with a magic marker: DIRTY DANCING near the light switch, SOS FOR LOVE near the bookshelf in which he kept his collection of teddy bears. A girl in Toronto keeps sending the bears, along with letters about flunking algebra and her screwed-up parents.

Before this year, Omar had been an outstanding student. His slide could be attributed partly to the government closures of his school in the Christian Quarter of Jerusalem. But part of it was something else. One night, Omar told Bassem he was "spinning around inside, all confused." He said he was tired of his friends, tired of talking about girls, music, videos. Lately, Omar had been hanging with college-age kids, talking politics, staying out to all hours. It used to be that Omar would sleep in Bassem's bed so that Bassem would have to wake him up when he came home from a night out. Now, Bassem was usually the one awake and waiting. He was worried that Omar would get himself arrested.

Where Omar was a private-school suburban, Bassem was a city streetwise. He'd been born in the kitchen of a house in the Old City, near the Damascus Gate, that his family had owned for two centuries. When he was still a little boy, he sold wooden camels, beaded rosaries. and brass menorahs to tourists from behind the counter in his family's shop. By the time he was twelve, he'd learned English, Hebrew, German, and some French, and he was hiring himself out as a personal tour guide. He'd wait around the Damascus Gate until he could pick up a family of tourists, preferably one with a pretty young daughter. He'd show them the Holy Sepulcher, the Arab souk, the Western Wall, the Dome of the Rock, chattering away about the mysteries and miracles of the Old City that he'd memorized from books. He never asked for money; he always came away with a generous tip. More recently, just before the Intifada, he had gone back into sales, specializing in fine Bedouin antiques.

Bassem had the gift of gab in many languages, especially Arabic, and when he walked through the streets of the Old City people waved and slapped his back. Once, a guy reached into my knapsack in the crowded market. Bassem called him by name, told him to lay off. I hadn't even noticed the hand in my bag. It was a tiny little village within the walled city. Bassem was a native son.

Bassem was the third of four brothers in a family of ten children. They had moved from the Old City to the Mount of Olives during the Six-Day War. One brother was studying psychology in London. A sister was married to an engineer and lived in Saudi Arabia. She visited rarely; permits were hard to obtain. All the rest of the grown children lived at home, in the way of most Arab families, which operate in communal fashion, each member giving what he can, each taking what he needs. One family under one roof. A tiny nation.

The roof, the home, is most important to Palestinians. In Islam, the land is the mother, and the mother is revered. It is she who carries on the generations, she who nurtures the present and the future. So too the house. When Palestinians build with concrete, they leave the top unfinished, steel rods exposed and waiting for the addition of the next floor. A Palestinian man's highest goal on earth is to house all of his family together. Out in the countryside, they build ranch-style, adding rooms, spreading out. In the city, they build apartment style, adding floors, moving up.

After his father died, Bassem's eldest brother became the head of the family. Assad favored $500 Hugo Boss sport coats, wore a Rolex watch. While I was visiting, he would twice travel to Germany on business. Each time he returned with a different German girl on his arm. The first one, the ex-wife of a West German bank robber, took a liking to Bassem. One night he borrowed my rental car and took her out on the town. After that, Bassem and his brother spoke even less frequently. Since their father died and Assad took charge, well... Bassem was a man of strong convictions. He didn't like being told what to do. He wanted to do what *he* wanted to do—that was his problem with Assad. It was also his problem with the State of Israel. To date, he'd been arrested seventeen times.

Between the ages of fourteen and thirty, Bassem said, he had spent a total of three years in prison, the longest stint being three months. He had been arrested for several barroom brawls with soldiers, all of them in Jewish West Jerusalem, all of them over girls Bassem was having drinks with. He'd also been arrested for throwing rocks, for throwing Molotov cocktails, for other reasons not specified in his records.

Though he remembers the Arab soldiers during the Jordanian occupation, and the fighting during the Six-Day War, Bassem's first personal memory of the Israeli occupation dates from age eleven. He'd been in his father's shop when word spread that a Jew had set off a bomb in the El Aqsa mosque.

"We heard of the bomb," Bassem remembers, "and everyone just ran through the market to the mosque. There is a big fire inside, and I see people carrying water to throw on the fire. And here I was carrying water too, not too much, just a small bucket, because I was small. I carried it and the big people would throw it. I mean, it was the mosque. I always prayed at this mosque when I was a kid. Of course I wanted to help to save it from the fire. Afterwards, you could see everybody in the Old City wearing black, everybody sad. You don't see anyone smiling around the city for a long time."

Bassem was thirteen the first time he witnessed the death of a friend. Mohammed was a champion bodybuilder in the West Bank. Tell a Palestinian father he has a handsome boy, and he won't be particularly pleased. Among Palestinians, the highest compliment you can give is "strong." Mohammed was the strongest of the strong, and he was a good guy, too. When Bassem would go lift weights at the gym in the Old City, "Mohammed would give me advises about what to do with my body."

Mohammed was in the act of throwing a stone when a soldier shot him in the head. "I was in shock," Bassem said. "It took me forty-eight hours even to talk. He was shot, and then we had to steal his body from the hospital. We stole it and walked it all around the city, and everyone came with us. His blood was on my shirt. Afterwards, we take his body to the mosque. I didn't want to go home, I wanted to be next to his body."

Within a year after Mohammed's death, Bassem was arrested for the first time. He was fourteen.

"One time there was a call over the loudspeakers at the mosque. There were Jewish people inside the mosque, trying to pray there. They claim this is their Second Temple and this is where they belonged.

"I answer the call, I come to the mosque. And I see one of them praying, one of these Jewish. And I jumped into him and I started to fight with him, and I catched him from the neck. I was strangling him. He was a bigger body than me, or even taller, and maybe over thirty years old. And then I started kicking him, and then there is the police catching me. I was really mad. I pushed the policeman and I tried to run away, but I wasn't lucky. I was caught.

"I stayed twenty-two days in jail before my trial. My mother, for twenty-two days, she never ate anything. She never smoked. All she did was drink coffee twenty-four hours a day and sit on the balcony waiting for me to come back. She was really upset. She refused to cook anything. She refused to let anyone turn on the television or even the radio.

"Among the Arabs, prison is something very bad. It means you have been stealing or killing or using drugs or all different bad things, bad things that dishonor your family. But the people in prison were OK. They talked about politics, about the Palestinian state. They told me listen, I should not be ashamed in prison. Being a political prisoner is something completely different. Being there gave me a clear picture of what it is meaning to live under occupation.

"They push you into a corner, the Israelis. This is the reason for the demonstrations. It is like a chain. It gets long and long and long, and this chain, it keeps going around your neck. And every time it's getting more tight and more tight. You know this is your homeland. You know you have the right to be here. You can't stand up and see people being shot in the street without doing anything, without feeling anything. If Gandhi himself was here, he would be turned into violence. Gandhi himself, honest to God. I mean, Palestinians have a hell of a life.

"How do you want me to feel? I want to live. Sometimes I really want to live. I want to go out there. I want to go to the beach. I want to be able to go out with a girl and have a good time. Maybe sometimes even you have a good time, but then you walk in the street and there is something else coming up to you to eat your heart, or even to eat your feelings, or even to fill you with lots of sorrows. You cannot enjoy a life like this. Always you know. Always you remember. To them we are a people who should not be here."

* * *

*Allahu akbar! Allahu akbar! Allahu akbar!*

We were in the middle of a riot.

Six hundred angry Palestinians, children and teens, mothers and fathers and grandparents, residents of a refugee camp in Gaza. They were throwing fists in the air and stamping their feet. They were yelling, "God is most great! God is most great!" The chords in their necks were straining, their eyes were fixed with hate.

Hatred for me.

Fingers were pointing, and then one finger was jabbing me in the chest, and then a hand pushed my left shoulder, and then another one pushed harder from the back and I almost lost my balance. A pebble hit the top of my head, a little pebble, arched from close range. And then a rock hit the hood of our car, and then another, and it sounded like the first drops before a heavy rain—tentative, pregnant, imminent...

Bassem and I were being kicked out of a refugee camp. It was the second time in two days.

Over the last month or so, members of the Shin Bet—Israel's internal security, the same people who'd greeted me at the airport—had been playing a little game in the territories. They'd been going into Palestinian cities, villages, and refugee camps in unmarked cars. They carried press cards and video cameras, posing as journalists. They'd interview people, the whole charade. They'd ask about throwing rocks, demonstrations, politics, friends. When the interviews were done, they'd make arrests.

News of these tactics had passed through military censors and was published in both Hebrew and Arabic newspapers. The government did not deny the story. Israel knew that as long as the Intifada stayed on the front page, world support would continue to deteriorate. Their hope was to turn the Palestinians against the press.

It appeared to be working.

Yesterday, in a village in the West Bank called Edna, Bassem and I had made friends with some *shebab*, the teenage soldiers of the Intifada. We'd spent all day with them, going from house to house, hearing the complaints, the laments, the litany of indignities and horrors heard in every camp and every city, the same stories out of different mouths, the same stories all the time.

The people of Edna were particularly strong in their faith in the Intifada. They were farmers and herders who lived in an ancient town built in the rolling hills near Hebron. Not long before I came, they'd managed to keep the soldiers out of their village of seventeen thousand for twenty-five days, repulsing the daily patrols of jeeps and trucks with rocks and molotovs. On the twenty-sixth day, according to the villagers, the army attacked with helicopters and paratroopers. The battle lasted six hours.

Edna, like most of its sisters in the West Bank, was a fortress camouflaged as a sleepy village. There was one main road in and out, littered with an obstacle course of boulders and mufflers and bed springs. Just before the first house, a large truck sat halfway across the road. As we came toward it, a small boy in the cab of the truck blew the horn. Three older boys then stepped out from behind. They questioned us. Bassem passed muster. One of them got in our car.

We drove slowly up the hill, toward the village proper. The *shebob* we'd picked up had his head out the window. He signaled his comrades on the rooftops, telling them to hold fire. Meanwhile, Bassem and I waved like two Shriners on a float. *"Alafi shebob!"* we called, over and over again. Hello guys!

Through the village, past the battlements, toward the town square. As we went, I thought about one of the *shebob* I'd met in the hospital in Nablus. His name was Faisal. He was studying to be a nurse. He'd wrestled a gun from a soldier, then slammed it onto the pavement, breaking the stock. Then he threw it down and ran. He'd been shot in the back.

I asked him why he didn't use the rifle to shoot the soldiers while he had the chance.

He shook his head, *tisk tisk.* "*They* shoot guns. *We* throw rocks. This is the point of Intifada," he had said.

It was this kind of simple, perverse, effective logic that had been the best ally of the Intifada since its beginnings. En masse, the Palestinians boycotted Israeli products, withheld taxes, stayed away from jobs in Israel. Palestinians who worked for Israel as tax collectors, civil servants, and police resigned their posts. Those who failed to resign, or who collaborated with the Israelis, were attacked or killed. Under the unofficial guidance of the United National Leadership of the Uprising in the Occupied Territories, known as the UNLU, the Palestinians were doing everything they could to pester, annoy, wear down, and piss off the Israelis. They couldn't overrun them, perhaps, but they could drive them to distraction, make them crazy like a man being swarmed by mosquitoes.

Over the months of the Intifada, in a series of numbered communiqués, UNLU had ordered flag days, days of fire, days of stones, days of sit-ins, days of demonstrations, days of commemorations, days of general strike. They'd asked merchants and professionals to lower their prices, organized food deliveries to curfewed villages, kept communications open between the territories. Though competition between factions in UNLU was becoming increasingly divisive, the people themselves were solid. Every Palestinian was linked in his or her desire for a homeland, and every one seemed to know the score: The illiterate goat herder in Gaza spoke passionately against American imperialism. The taxi driver in the West Bank derided the military industrial complex. The mother in the refugee camp complained of the influence of New York Jews on American government policy. They were a nation of people exceedingly attuned to current events. A nation of people with one goal: a homeland.

In Edna, Bassem and I had gotten as far as being assigned a room for the night. Then, as the daylight faded, a throng of *shebob* gathered outside the house. One of them told my host that I looked like an Israeli settler he'd seen once, a guy with a shaved head and a beard.

And that was that. We were escorted out of town.

The next day, we saddled up for Gaza.

Thus far, over the past five weeks, my travels with Bassem had taken us all over the country, from the ancient Arab coastal city of Akko to the Dead Sea, the lowest point on earth; from the West Bank to Gaza; from

Bethlehem to Beersheba; from the Golan Heights to the Egyptian border. I'd met Mohammed, the graduate of Bethlehem University School of Hotel management, and Nasser, the civil engineer. I'd made rounds at a hospital in Ramallah with Dr. Jibril, the urologist, toured Nablus with his brother, a lawyer. We'd been in many places, met many people. But always, as night fell, the hospitality would dry up like the sludge at the bottom of a cup of Turkish coffee, and we'd be ushered out of town.

Always, as we left, we'd see soldiers marching in.

Everywhere we went, the Palestinians told of the horrors of the night. But no one would let me stay to witness. They were afraid what would happen if the soldiers found us in their house. They were afraid we knew the soldiers. They would talk to us for a little while, but they wouldn't let us into their lives, and I guess I didn't blame them. They didn't know who I was. I had two press cards, but one of them was written in Hebrew. I was suspect. Everyone kept saying I looked like a Jew. I wondered what Bassem thought.

Bassem had a Bedouin friend named Ziad who lived in Khan Yunis, near Gaza. Ziad had a friend who had some friends in the Beach Camp, known locally as the Shati camp, a teeming complex along the wide, sandy coast of the Mediterranean. Built originally in 1948 to house some twenty-three thousand Palestinians—refugees who were displaced from their homes by the creation of the Jewish state and the ensuing war. Forty years later, the camp held upwards of one hundred thousand people including several generations of Palestinians who had known no other home.

Ziad's friend Samir was the one who had contacts in the Beach Camp. His seventeen-year-old Peugeot plowed through the deep sand like a 4×4. Just outside the camp, about a half mile shy of the checkpoint, he turned a quick left onto a donkey path.

The sand in the camp was particularly deep, and it was black, the color of burnt tires. Sewage flowed at speed toward the sea in open, foot-wide trenches. Garbage in the streets festered in 115-degree heat. Electric wires hung overhead—the wires themselves were hung with illegal Palestinian flags, American-made tear gas canisters, pairs of old athletic shoes. The houses, built of crumbling concrete and mud—some large and approaching grand, some merely shacks—had high walls and open courtyards, were huddled together haphazardly on narrow lanes that spilled, eventually, into a large central field of sand.

I was slumped down in the back of the Peugeot. Samir turned into one of the lanes, pulled in front of a small house, and stopped. We were hurried to a back room. The walls and roof were made of tin. It felt like an oven.

We sat on carpets on the floor, drank coffee, smoked cigarettes. Samir and his friend talked and argued a while, and then the friend left. He returned with a plastic bag. The substance inside was black and gummy. It was passed around in a gesture of friendship. Everyone took a little on the tip of a match stick. You sucked a while, and then chewed. It was gritty and sour, tasted like tar. Then you washed it down with the coffee.

The talk continued. More coffee was served. As usual, not knowing the language, I felt a little bit left out. I looked around the room, tried to make eye contact, tried to follow what was being said. By now, after more than a month in the occupied territories, I could pretty well catch the drift of the conversation—the tones and the gestures, the body language, the occasional proper noun, the look in people's eyes.

Usually in these negotiations—there had been many over the weeks—I would sit this way and listen for while until I got the feeling that it was time for me to speak for myself. (Though I sometimes wondered who was truly in charge of this little journalistic enterprise, I couldn't let Bassem do *everything*. After all, *I* was the reporter.) For shorthand we started calling it the The Big Close.

Giving The Big Close, I would speak and gesture forcefully, the way the Arabs did. Sentence for sentence, Bassem would translate. I'd tell them that I was not an Israeli, that I was not a Shin Bet, that I was not, gulp, a Jewish. I'd tell them that I was looking only to see the truth with my own eyes, that I didn't want to hurt anyone, that I wouldn't take any names. I'd tell them about the one million American readers who would get my story on their front porch on some future Sunday morning—important people, senators and congressmen, even the president. And I'd tell them how public opinion was turning. I'd tell them that American Jews were not as powerful and popular with the leading American WASPs as they might think. It was a helluva speech; it came from my heart. It had gotten us *this* close...

Now, sitting in the hot tin shed, a bit woozy from the opium, I felt it was time to get to The Big Close. We'd come a long way. I'd been here five weeks. My expense account was totally gone; at this point I was pretty far into what I was hoping would be my fee. I reached over, knocked Bassem on the knee. I whispered in his ear, "Ready for The Big Close?"

No response.

I shook his shoulder. "Bassem?"

Slowly, his face turned in my direction. Both of his eyes were fixed and unfocused. His pupils were pinholes. His complexion was an alarming shade of olive green. "I think I need some water," he said in English, and then he said something in Arabic. Our host led him out of the room.

The talk continued around me. I had no idea what was going on. Then, from just outside the shed, I heard a thud. It was a sickening sound, like a side of beef falling onto a concrete floor. A moment later, our host dragged Bassem through the door, feet first. He was out cold.

At first I didn't move. I was a stranger, a white American stranger. One thing I've learned over the years is that in a situation like this, in a place like this, you can't act like a know-it-all. Through the history of Colonialism, white people have always acted that way. We can see now where this has gotten us. I was alone in a refugee camp without any translator. The best thing to do was to show deference, to be cool. They were men. This was their home. They knew what they were doing. They'd take care of Bassem, I was sure.

Our host set Bassem in a heap against the wall, placed an electric fan next to him. Then he took his old seat in the circle, resumed partying.

The fan oscillated back and forth. In the dim light of the shed, it appeared that Bassem's lips were beginning to turn blue.

In a little while I had him on his feet and walking, and now he was sitting next to me, semialert and semicoherent. Everyone was smiling at me, like I was Florence Nightingale, and I was feeling pretty good. Surely this would convince them I wasn't Shin Bet. Surely this was proof of my good intentions.

"Bassem," I whispered.

"Yesssss, Miiiike."

"Could you try the Big Close now?"

Just then two men entered. A discussion ensued. Bassem was not really operational. I gathered from the gestures that they wanted me to meet some people in the camp, some elders, perhaps. That was fine with me. I had nothing to hide. I followed them out of the room, alongside a house, toward the dusty street.

A crowd had gathered. One of them spoke to me in English. "May I see your press card please?"

His name was Sharif. He worked as a stringer for a news organization, he said. He'd of course heard of the

*Washington Post*. He showed me his own press card. I mentioned some names of Palestinian journalists I'd met in Jerusalem. I mentioned Dr. Jibril. I mentioned the lawyer. He knew them all.

"Come," Sharif said. "They want you to walk around the camp. The people want to see you, then maybe you can stay."

We walked down the lane toward the large central field. Samir and Ziad followed in the Peugeot. As we walked, more and more people joined the procession. Behind the car, Bassem walked with the help of a pair of *shebob*, each holding an arm.

As we reached the central field, the crowd gathered and grew. Hundreds of faces surrounded me, pushing closer, laughing and shouting and pointing. Then one of the kids yelled out "Shamir," the name of the Israeli prime minister, and everyone stamped on the ground and pointed their thumbs down. Someone else yelled "Reagan." Someone else yelled "Shultz." They stamped their feet. They pointed down.

I got the picture: I did the same.

I stamped and thumbed down. I made a terrible face. Everyone cheered.

Then someone put a Palestinian flag in my hand. It was homesewn, a triangle of red, green and white—the outlawed flag of the PLO, in my hand. I could be shot just for holding it. I wondered if the soldiers at the checkpoint had heard the ruckus and were on their way. Everyone around me was silent. What would the journalist do now?

I did what I had to do. I raised the flag, this illegal PLO flag. I raised it high in the air, raised it repeatedly, punched it up there as convincingly as I could, like some demented bald-headed cheerleader. I screamed at the top of my lungs: "PALESTINE! ALLLLL-RIGHT! PALESTINE! YEAHHHHH! PALEEEEEEESTIIIIIIINE!!!!!!"

They screamed. They squealed. They loved it!

They began chanting my name: "Mike! Mike! Mike! Mike!"

It was beautiful. I was in. Finally, we'd made it.

And then in the middle distance, I became aware of another chant.

*Allahu akbar! Allahu akbar! Allahu akbar!*

I had won over *this* group, yes. But word of a Jewish interloper had already spread through the camp like a wildfire. They hadn't seen my flag bit. They hadn't heard the chant: "Mike Mike Mike!"

I looked up across the sandy field. People were pouring out from every lane, from every direction, coming at me fast across the open plaza, hundreds of them, with stones in their hands, a full-blown riot, *Allahu akbar! Allahu akbar! Allahu akbar!*

A pebble hit my head. A rock hit the car.

"I'm very sorry," Sharif said. He pushed me from behind, hurrying me toward the vehicle. "Perhaps you can come back again. I'm very sorry."

I jumped in, slammed the door. The starter ground.

Finally, it caught. Samir began to pull away.

"Wait!" I said. "Where's Bassem?"

Samir kept rolling, very slowly through the crowd. They were banging on the car. I banged Samir on the shoulder. "We have to get Bassem!"

I jumped out. Samir stopped the car. I raised my palms in submission to the mob. "It's ok. It's ok. We're going," I said, pointing toward the exit. "I just want to get my friend."

They let Bassem pass. He had a loopy grin on his face. I piled him into the back seat and Samir floored it, fishtailing though the sand in hail of stones.

Outside the camp, a collective nervous laugh spread through the car. Samir switched on his lights, made a slow U-turn to avoid the military checkpoint.

Suddenly, a bright spotlight.

Israeli soldiers.

We'd been spotted.

\* \* \*

Bassem is calling, collect from Stuttgart.

"I called my lawyer back in Jerusalem," he says. "She say to me, 'Bassem stay where you are.' "

"What does that mean?"

"Well Mike, they have arrested eighty people from Jerusalem, and already eighteen of them are people I really know."

"It says in the newspaper that the Israelis have been rounding up organizers of the Intifada. Are they saying you're an organizer?"

"Yes, they believe I am."

"Why?"

"I don't know. This is what I need to find out. I have to wait for the court cases of the ones already arrested. Especially two certain people."

"Wait a minute. Do you think they really have something on you?"

"I don't know."

"Is there something to have?"

"Well... "

"Bassem."

"Yes there is, Mike."

"For organizing things?"

"Well, I used to know a few leaders. I used to sit with them. You know—"

"Go on."

"Well... We used to do these things. Writing the papers, the leaflets, saying when there is a strike, saying what is good for the people to do, you know, discussing what times the shops would open, or even not to have them open at all."

"You were one of the organizers?"

"Yesssss, Miiiike."

\* \* \*

While we were in Gaza, trying to get into the camp, Bassem's little brother, Omar, had been studying for finals. All across the city, kids were cramming in groups, trying to make up for time lost to the Intifada began. Since December, the government had closed schools for a total of four months.

On Tuesday, the day we'd left, one of Omar's class-mates, a boy named Nidal, had peddled his bicycle from his house in the Old City to a well-to-do Arab suburb just outside Jerusalem, to study with some friends.

According to press reports, Nidal was returning home when some kids threw rocks at a bus. On the bus were six armed men—three soldiers, three civilians. According to eyewitnesses, after the bus was pelted, the driver pulled over. The armed men jumped out of the bus and laid down fire. Both the Jerusalem Police and the army denied any involvement. Nidal was killed.

Omar was heartbroken. He'd known Nidal all his life. After a sleepless night, Omar went to see another friend from school, Faisal. They knocked around for a while, then decided to go to a photo shop in the Old City and have their picture taken together. Palestinian boys and men are very close. From a young age, in Islamic culture, males and females are seperated. In a family's house, the boys have a room, the girls have a room. Men eat with men, hang out with men, sleep in a room with men. Younger men serve older men. Older boys take care of younger boys. Neighbors and cousins are always around. Palestinian men hold hands, lock arms, rest a hand on each other's knees or thighs. It's not sexual. It's affection. They grow up together. Their feelings are very strong.

To reaffirm their feelings, to soften their grief, Omar and Faisal went to the photo store in the Old City. The man gave them the choice of several different backdrops. They almost chose the tropical beach with palm trees. In the end, they settled upon the alpine forest; they sat on a bench and held hands.

Then, as luck would have it, on the way out of the shop, they ran into the middle of the demonstration that had been called to protest Nidal's death.

Now, Omar had been in jail for two days. Bassem was beside himself. His mother was hysterical. She cried and cried. She washed all the floors twice, slamming a rag mop across the tile. We had no idea where exactly Omar was, or whether he was injured, or whether he'd been beaten. We had no idea about anything concerning Omar. All we knew were the possibilities.

"When I was there," said Bassem, "they didn't torture me every day. Just every few days. They'd put this sack on your head, a really rotten sack with shit in it. Or they'd put those handcuffs on your hands behind your back, or even you are hanging from the wall, half standing, half sitting, with your hands tied behind your back and then tied to the wall. And sometimes they put you in a cold shower when it's really cold, and then they put you in front of an air conditioner.

"You're in your cell, and they put you into psychology things. You never know when they're going to come. Maybe late at night, or maybe in the morning, or maybe not at all this day. First they will sweet-talk you, these sweet sugar words, making you to feel safe. Then another guy wants to beat you up, jump on you, or he says, 'we will screw your mother, we will screw your sister,' we will do this, do that."

\* \* \*

Outside the jail, in the Russian Compound in Jerusalem, we waited for word of Omar. Bassem was sitting on the steps, Assad was standing behind him, wearing a chic, six-button blazer in the stultifying heat. Their mother was holding a place in a long line outside a metal door.

At eye level in the door was a window with a sliding cover. The man at the head of the line kept inching open the cover, trying to steal a look inside. He'd open it slowly, stealthily, one millimeter at a time. Then someone inside would slam it shut. Then he'd start again. Like everyone else in line, he clutched in his free hand a little slip of blue paper, a permit to bring clothes and food to a loved one being held without charges in jail.

Occasionally, the guard, a very large man in uniform, would open the door. He'd inspect a bag, ask a name, take the bag inside, close the door again. Sometimes he'd decide that two apples had to be taken out of a bag. Or that grapes were OK, but bananas were not. Or that all the food in *this* paper bag had to be placed in *that* plastic bag.

It was late in the afternoon. We had spent the morning going from one office to the next. From the Old City to the Russian Compound. From the jail to the lawyer. From the press office to the office of the chief of police. A maze of offices, a shroud of runaround. We weren't asking for much. We just wanted to know where Omar was. We wanted to know what he was charged with. We wanted to visit him or get him a lawyer.

They would tell us nothing.

It would go like this:

"I need a permit to visit my brother."

"We don't know anything about your brother. We don't handle the young ones."

Two officers walk by, escorting a teenager in handcuffs.

"Listen," said Bassem, "if you want to play this game with me, go and come. Just say it to me."

"OK," the man said. "I will. Maybe I can help."

"Yes?"

"On one condition. All I need is for your brother to sign a paper—"

"Forget it!"

We ran around and around and around. No one would help. I became outraged and got into it, too. I took my American citizenship and my press card and went from office to office to office. I wanted to know the policy on press visiting prisoners. A simple question. "What is the policy?"

Rivka in the government press office sent me to the chief of police's office. Both of his spokesmen were unavailable. They sent me to another office. They sent me somewhere else. I ended up in the tourist complaint center. "Please wait," they said.

So now we were waiting in line with a permit for food, something anyone could get. Perhaps that way we could at least confirm that Omar was here. Every twenty minutes or so the guard would take in a package. Every so often, the metal door would open and a couple of agents would escort a couple of boys in handcuffs out of the door, across the compound, to the police station to be booked.

At four in the afternoon, the guard opened the door again. *Masalami*, he announced, smiling sadistically. "Goodbye, all." Then he closed the door. The lock clicked.

Nobody budged. Bassem's mother tapped her high-heeled foot. Assad chewed his moustache. Bassem lit a cigarette.

"You know, Mike," he said, exhaling, "this Intifada is going to last for a long time. Here we are. Fighting against weapons, fighting against everybody. Nobody's helping, but it's OK, it's really OK. We have a saying in Arabic: nothing can scratch your skin except your own nail. You know, no one is going to scratch your skin for you. And this is the Palestinians. I mean, the Palestinians are not waiting for Jordan to make a war against Israel because they know it will never happen. They know Saudi Arabia will never stop the oil and say to the Americans, 'Listen, if you want the oil, give the Palestinians a state.' We know these things will never happen.

"It doesn't matter. I'm one of the people who believe that if I want to grow an olive tree in the garden, I have to wait at least five years to get an olive. You know, after taking care of this tree, looking after it, taking really good care, this tree would start giving me olives. But then for the next years in my life it would keep giving me olives. And even for my grand-grandchildren. When ever you go around any Palestinian village, you will see a lot of olives. Olive is a very patient tree. It is the tree of the Palestinian people."

Fifteen minutes passed. Twenty-five. A half hour. We waited. For what I didn't know.

Then, behind us, the metal door opened. Everyone turned their heads.

Two agents exited, followed by two boys in handcuffs, followed by two more agents. They moved past us, toward the parking lot.

Omar!

We stood—Bassem, Assad, Mom and me—glued to our different positions. The back of Omar's shirt was torn. His pants were dirty. His hair was uncombed.

Bassem dropped his bag of fruit and dashed across the parking lot toward Omar. Assad took off after him.

The distance between them closed. Thirty yards, twenty, ten. As he ran, Bassem reached inside his shirt and pulled out... a Cadbury chocolate bar. He tore off the wrapper.

Dodging an agent, Bassem leapt for Omar, shoved the candy into his little brother's mouth. Another agent caught him with fist behind the ear. Down he went.

Assad was right behind with a banana. One of the agents knocked it from his hand, punched him in the stomach. He crumpled.

I ran to them and knelt helplessly—Assad fetal, Bassem on his back. I looked up in time to see Omar's back recede, his arms pinioned by two agents. Omar's head was held high. He was strutting.

\* \* \*

I was in my room, packing my bags. It was two a. m. I had to be at the airport at four, leaving enough time for the inevitable search and questioning. Bassem slouched in the armchair beside the bed. As a present, he had brought me a *jalabia*, a long, silk shirt-dress. Every Palestinian man had at least one.

"I have something to tell you, Bassem."

"What?"

"Have you figured it out yet? About me?"

"What?"

"I'm Jewish."

He regarded me a moment. Then he said, somewhat triumphantly, "I knew you were a Jewish."

"You knew?"

"Come on, Mike, you have a Jewish name."

"I do?"

"Assad said this. Ziad said this. It is no surprise."

"It doesn't matter?"

"No. I don't give a damn shit."

"You're sure? I mean, I feel… "

"Listen Mike," he said, looking deeply into my eyes, "If you first iron that *jalabia* before you wear it, it will look very nice. I know that all the womens at home will be falling all over you."

\* \* \*

Bassem is calling, collect from Stuttgart.

"The people here are very boring here, very cold," he says. "Everything is like a computer. There is no excitement in the life."

"That's because there are no Israeli soldiers."

"At least at home, I used to have an argument every day with a soldier! They ask me for my Identicard. They stop me at checkpoints. They bother me. I get mad. I get used to this!"

"Maybe you'll get used to Germany. Maybe things will get better."

"Maybe. There are one hundred maybes in this world, Mike. There's one hundred maybes. Maybe maybe maybe. It's far away from reality."

"Bassem, you have to try."

"Here I am so isolated. You hear nothings about Jerusalem, nothings about the West Bank or Gaza. I went all over Stuttgart and I finally found a newspaper in Arabic. It was three days old. Six people were shot, one person was killed in the Beach Camp, seventy-five people released, another hundred people was arrested. The usual game they always play.

"I want to go back. Soon as I can. Soon as I see everythings clear out in front of me. Now if it's four years in prison, I'll go back. I'll spend those four years. At least you know you are in your home. At least you know you are there. That's it. To me, four years, five years, I can do it.

"You'd rather go back home and go to prison?"

"Yesssssss, Miiiiike."

# *About the Author*

MIKE SAGER is a best-selling author and award-winning reporter. A former Washington Post staff writer under Watergate investigator Bob Woodward, he worked closely, during his years as a contributing editor to Rolling Stone, with gonzo journalist Hunter S. Thompson. Sager is the author of 6 collections of non-fiction, two novels, and one biography. He has served for more than fifteen years as a writer at large for Esquire. In 2010 he won the American Society of Magazine Editors' National Magazine Award for profile writing for his article "The Man Who Never Was". Many of his stories have been optioned for film. For more information, please see www.mikesager.com.

# About the Publisher

THE SAGER GROUP was founded in 1984 by author and journalist Mike Sager. In 2012 it was chartered as a multimedia artists' and writers' consortium, with the intent of empowering those who make art—an umbrella beneath which makers can pursue, and profit from, their craft directly, without gatekeepers. TSG publishes eBooks and paper books; manages musical acts and produces live shows; ministers to artists and provides modest grants; and produces and distributes documentary, feature and web-based films. By harnessing the means of production, The Sager Group helps artists help themselves. For more information, please see www.TheSagerGroup.Net.

www.ingramcontent.com/pod-product-compliance
Lightning Source LLC
Chambersburg PA
CBHW021941040426
42448CB00008B/1182